If You Give A Dog A Doobie

Again for Ariel and Sam
-S.M.

Again for Aurora
-M.O.

Special Thanks To:

Tosca Miserendino

Stacie Odum

Jack W. Perry

Don Loudon

Ron Riffle

Beverly Miserendino

Travis Bundy

Shawn Gates

Joao Pimentel

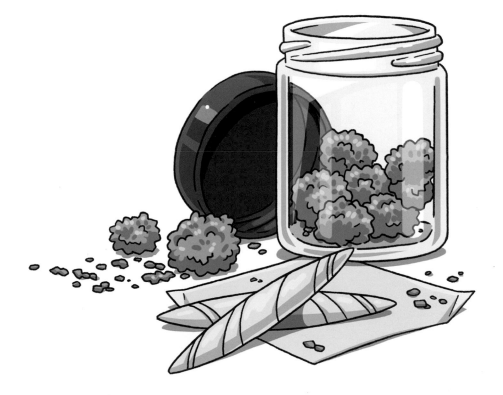

If You Give A Dog A Doobie

Written By **Sam Miserendino**

Illustrated By **Mike Odum**

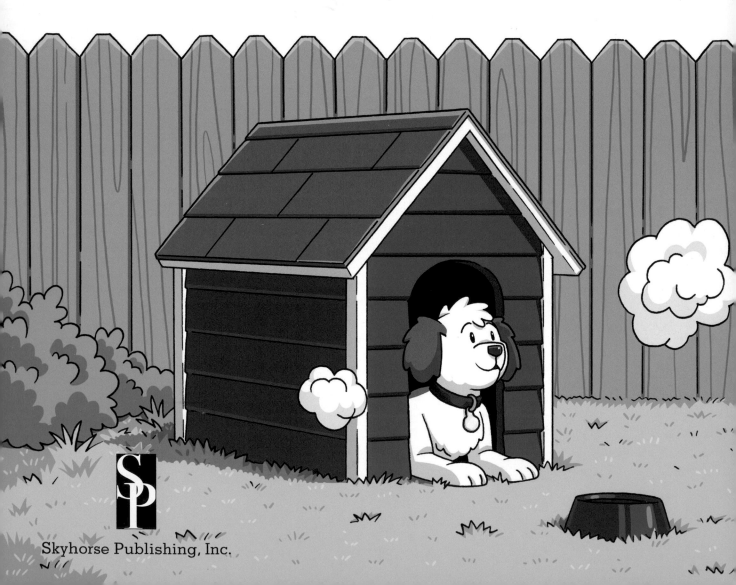

Skyhorse Publishing, Inc.

KRUNCHY KREME

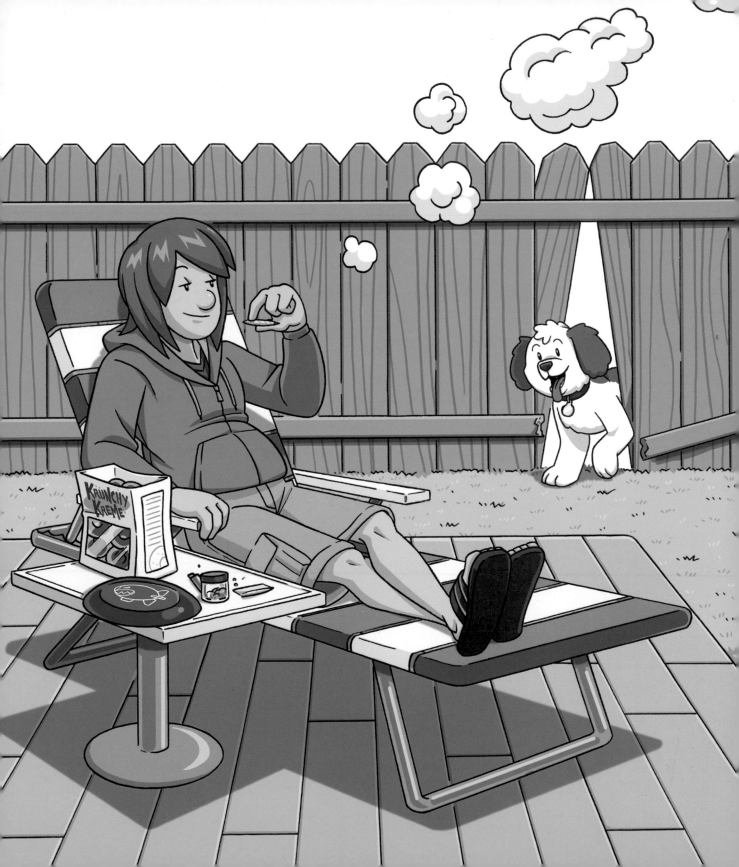

If you give a dog a doobie, he'll ask
you if there's chocolate in it.

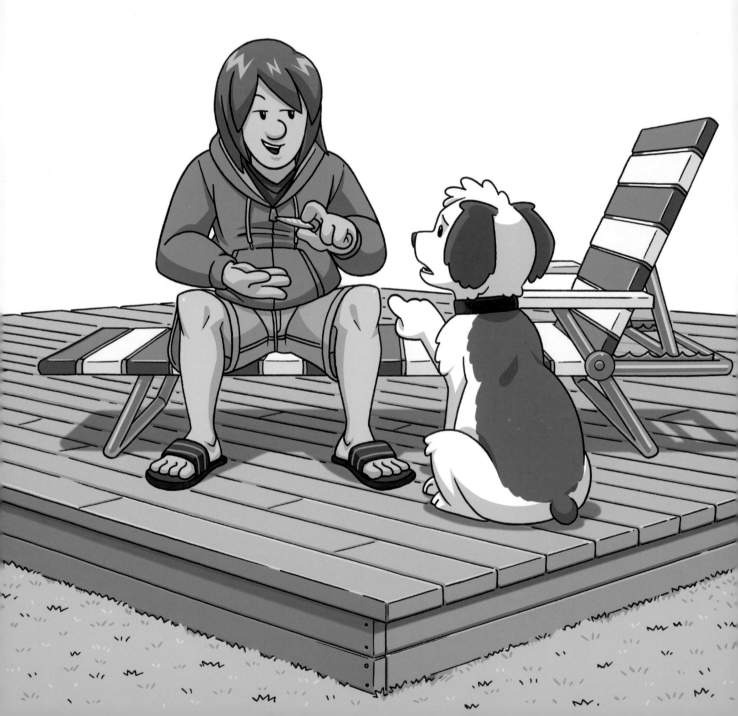

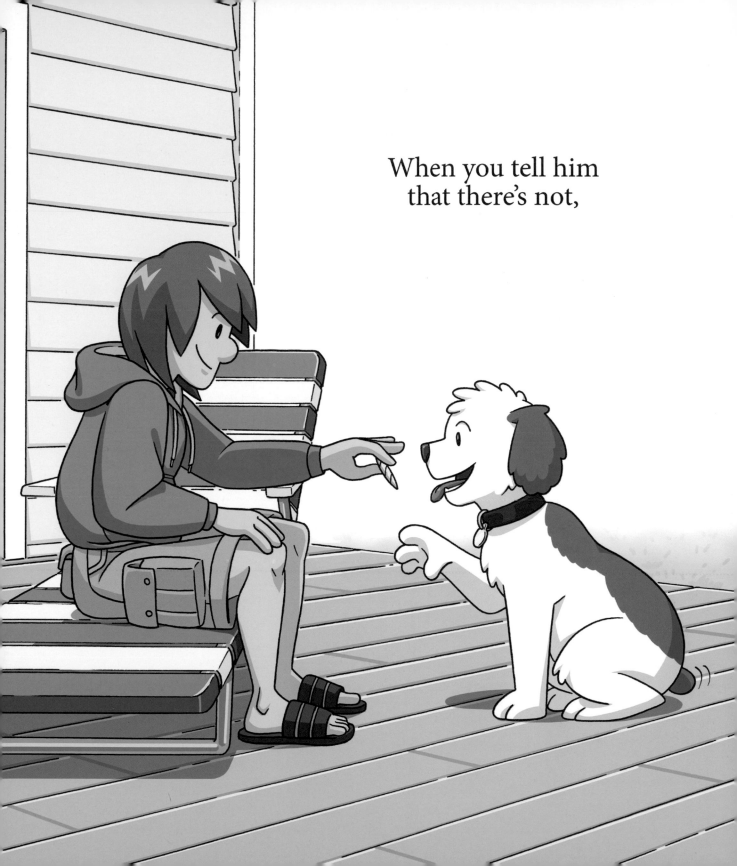

When you tell him
that there's not,

he'll puff...

Puff…

And...uh,
you'll pass.

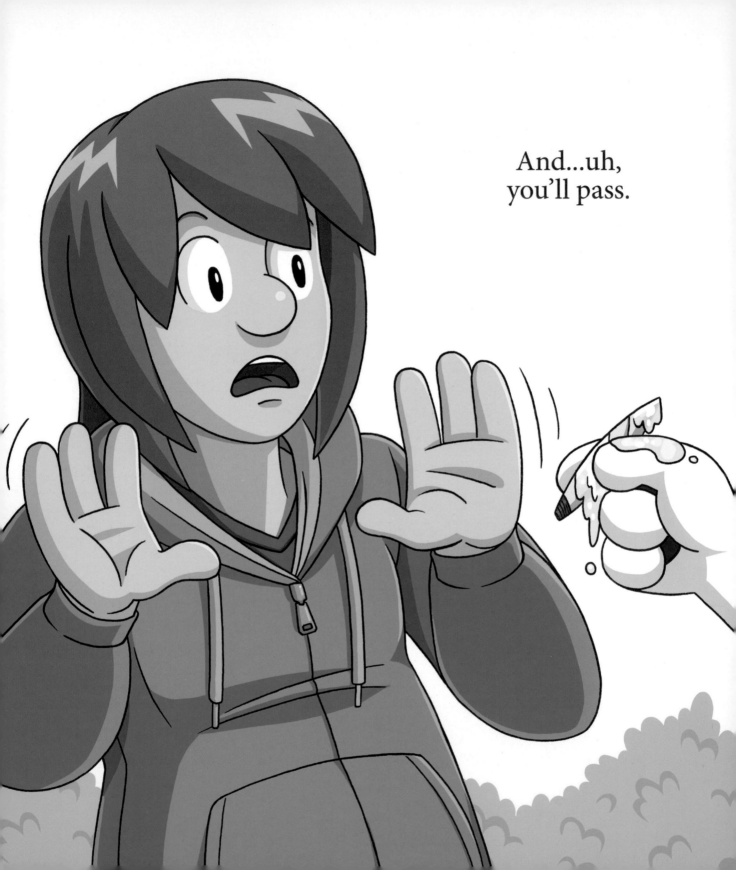

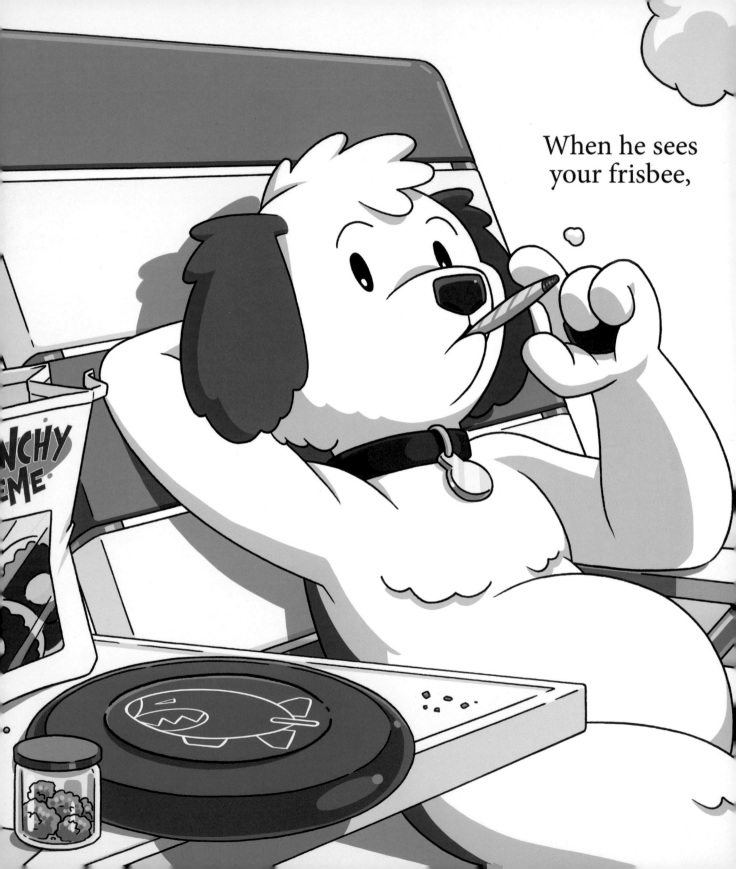

When he sees
your frisbee,

he'll ask you to throw
it to him.

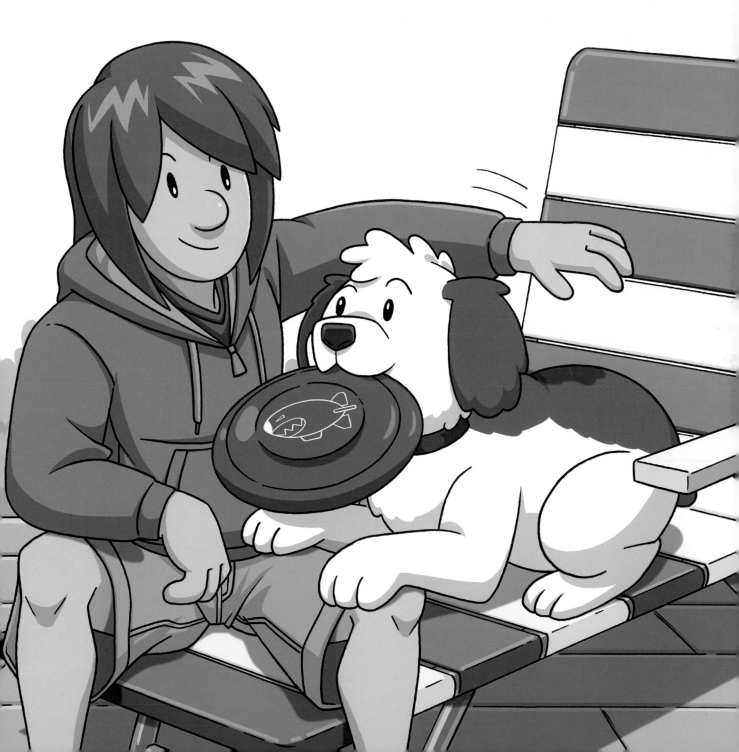

He'll feel like he's soaring...

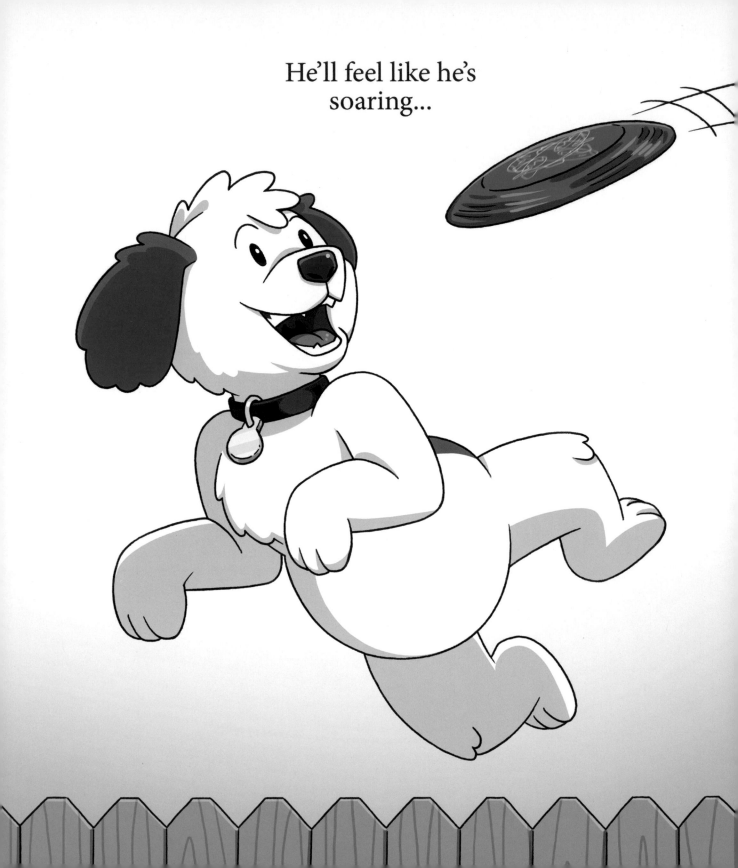

But he's not.

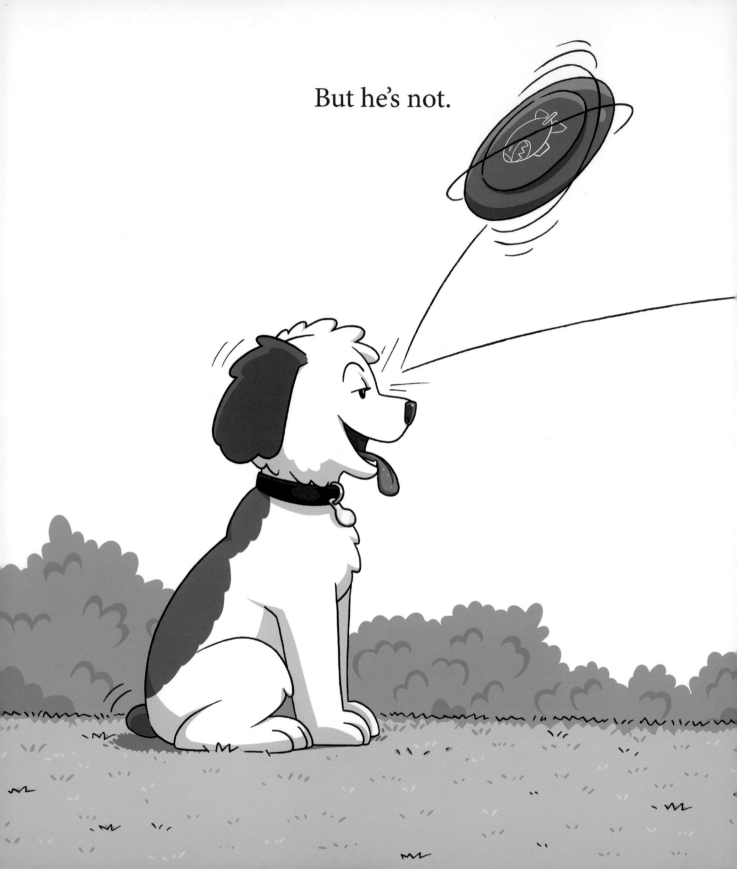

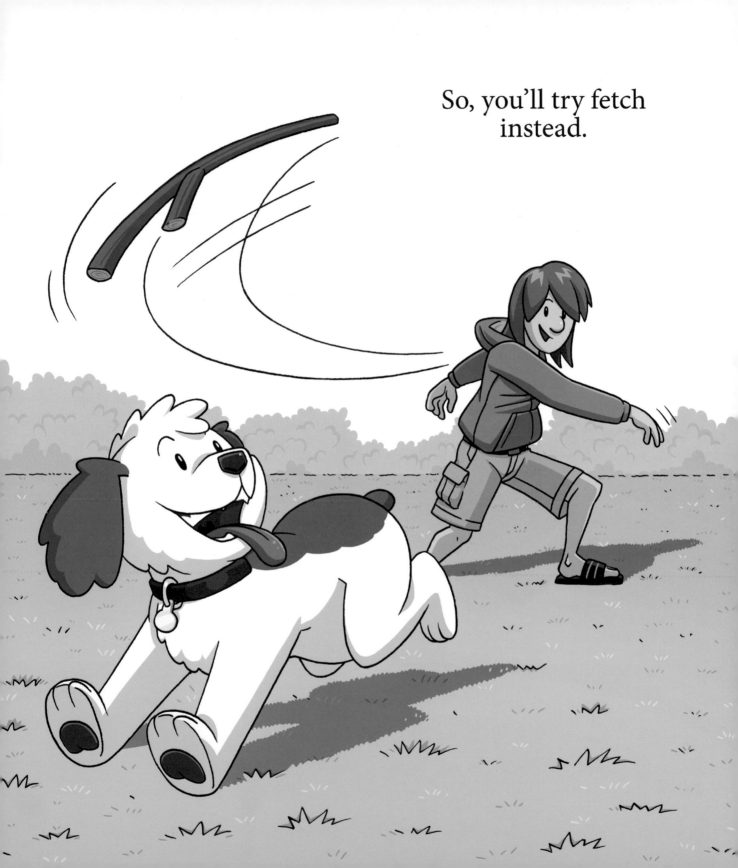

So, you'll try fetch instead.

When he gets to where
the stick landed,

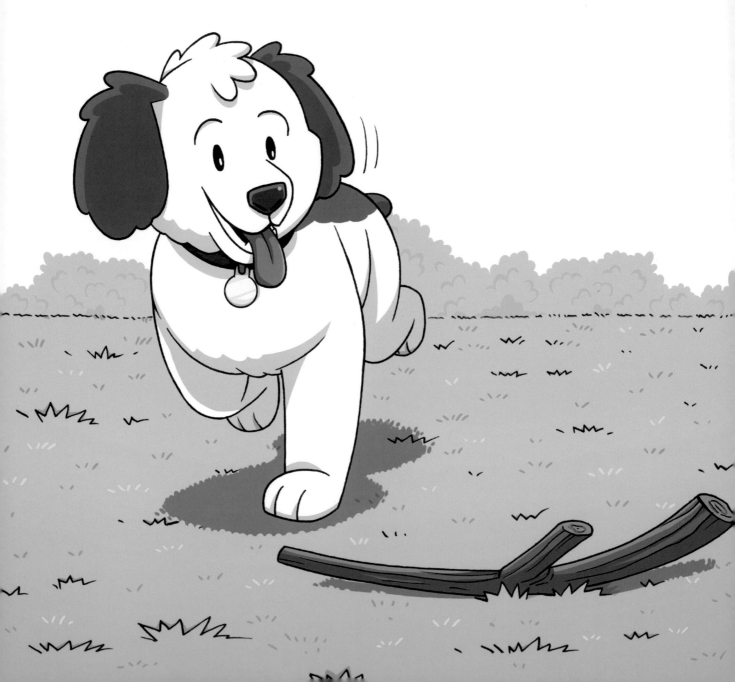

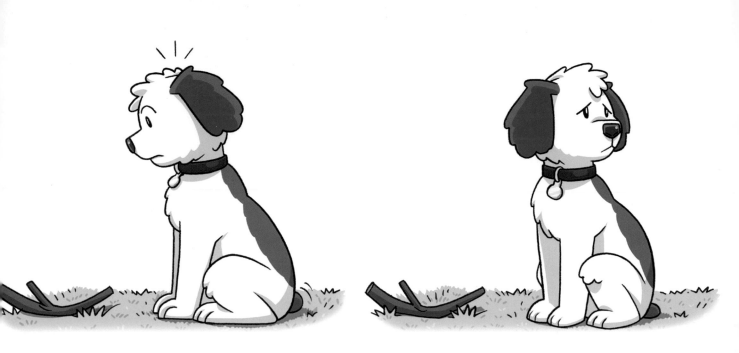

he'll try to remember
why he's there…

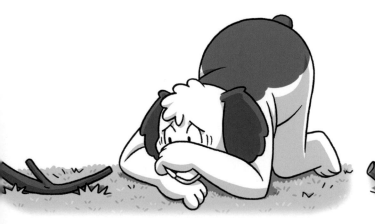

But he can't.

Then you'll ask him what tricks he can do, and he'll tell you he can play dead...

Not only that,
he can roll over...

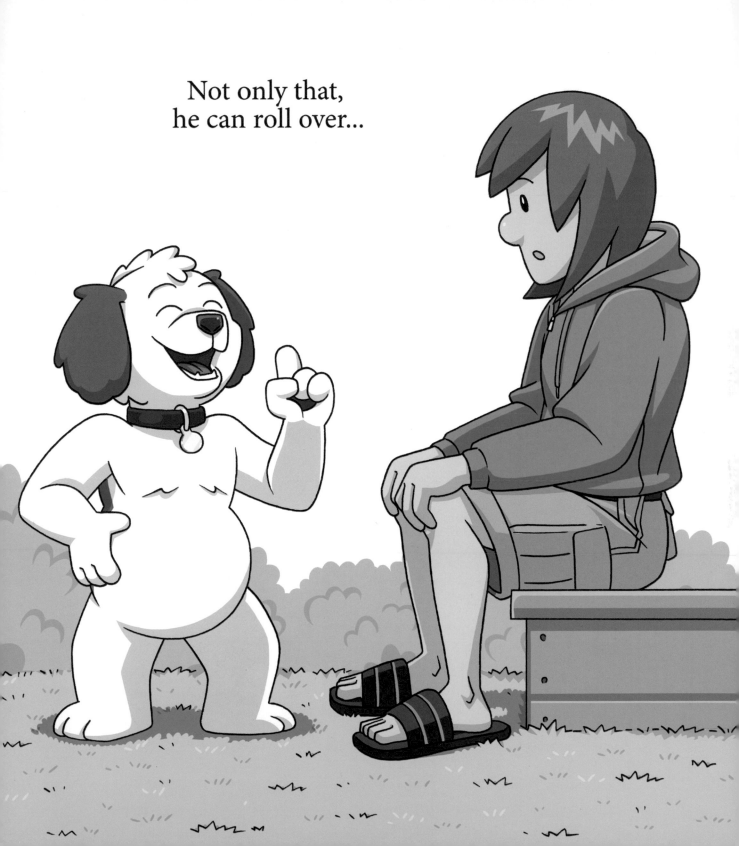

And over...

And over...

And he'll keep rolling, until...

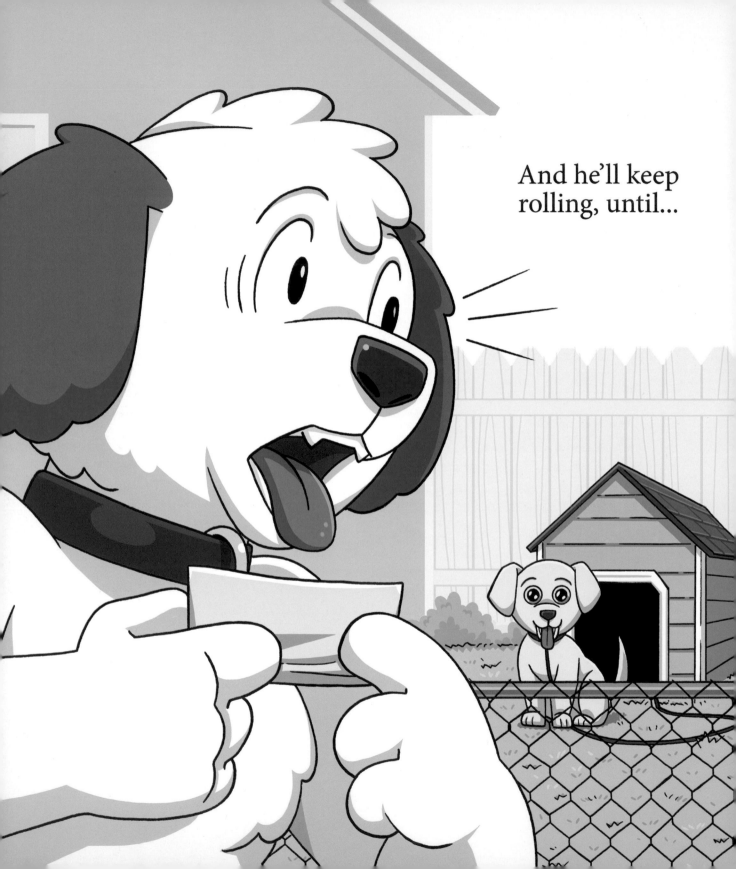

He'll tell you he's sure
the dog next door is an
undercover K-9,

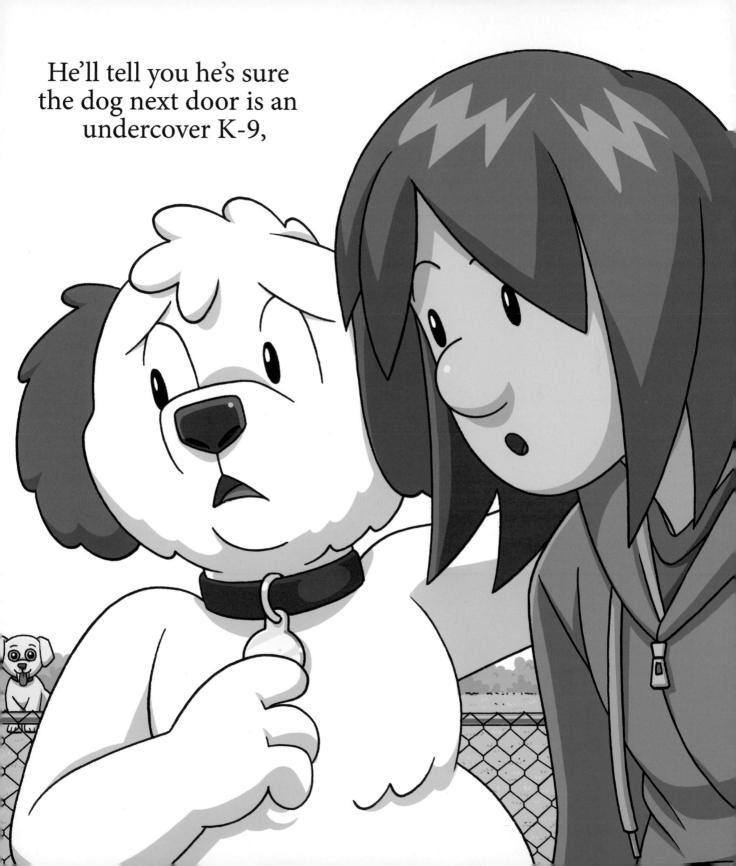

and that the two of you should slowly walk into the house...real slow...like nothing's wrong.

Once you're in the house,
he'll tell you that was close...

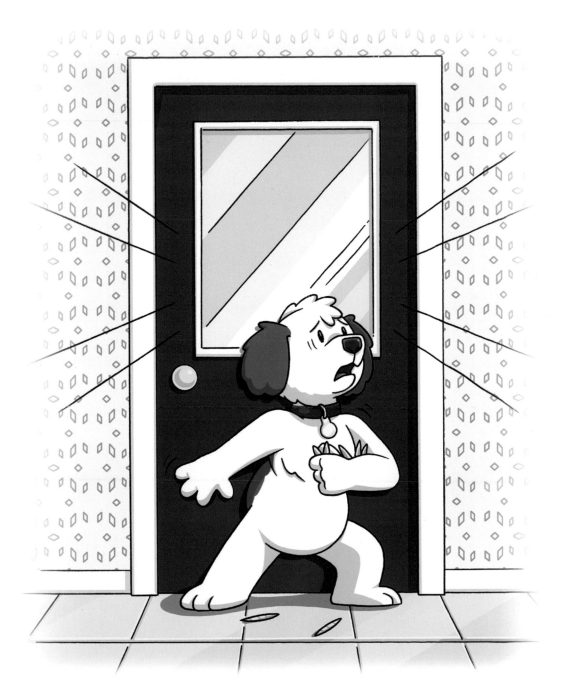

too close...

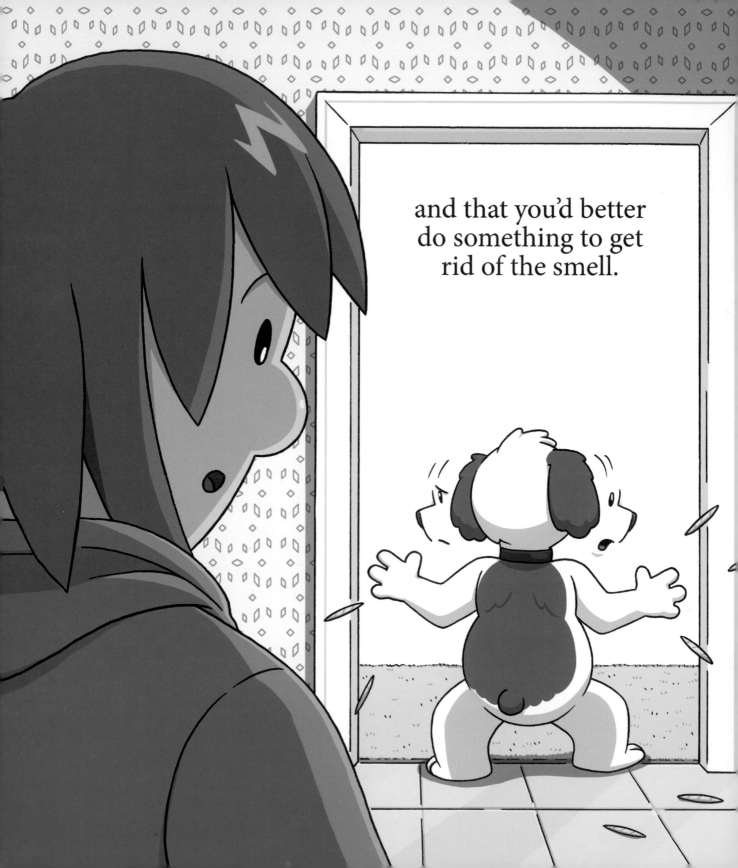

and that you'd better do something to get rid of the smell.

So, he'll rub...   And rub...

And rub...

Until...

he sees his tail!

He’ll chase
his tail...

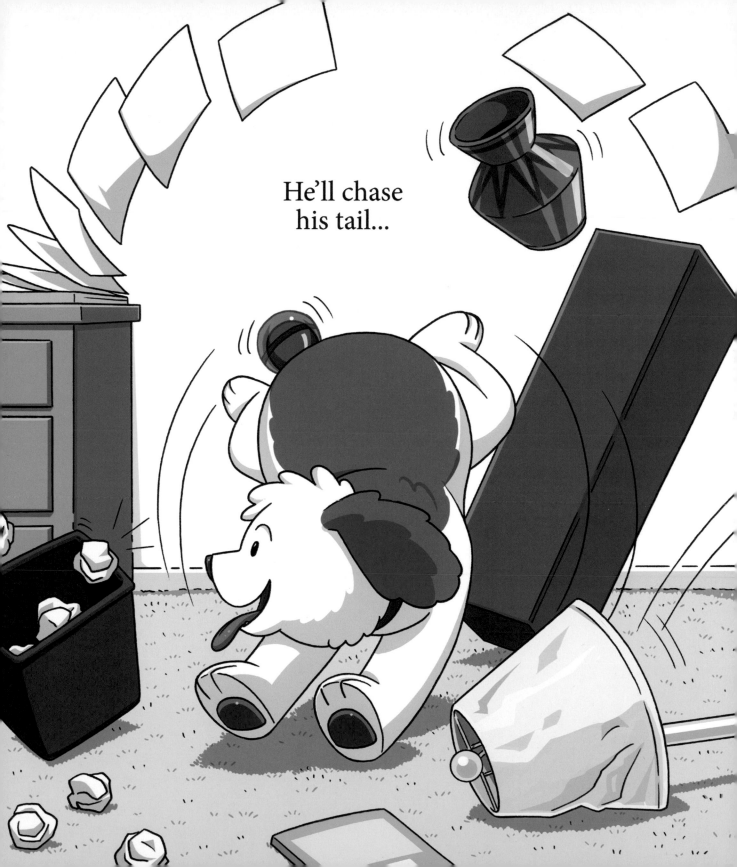

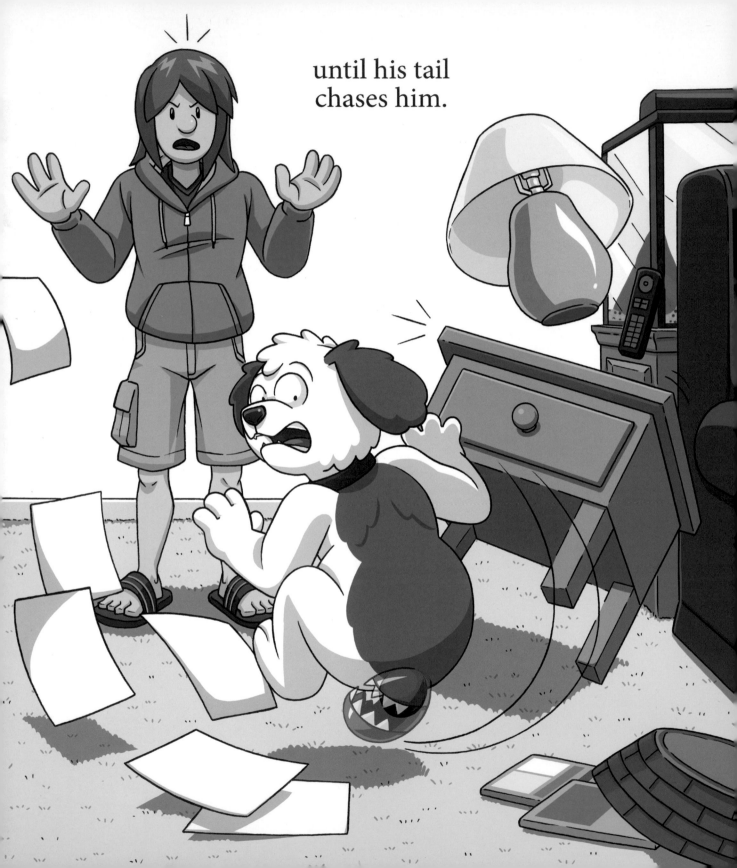

until his tail
chases him.

When it's over,

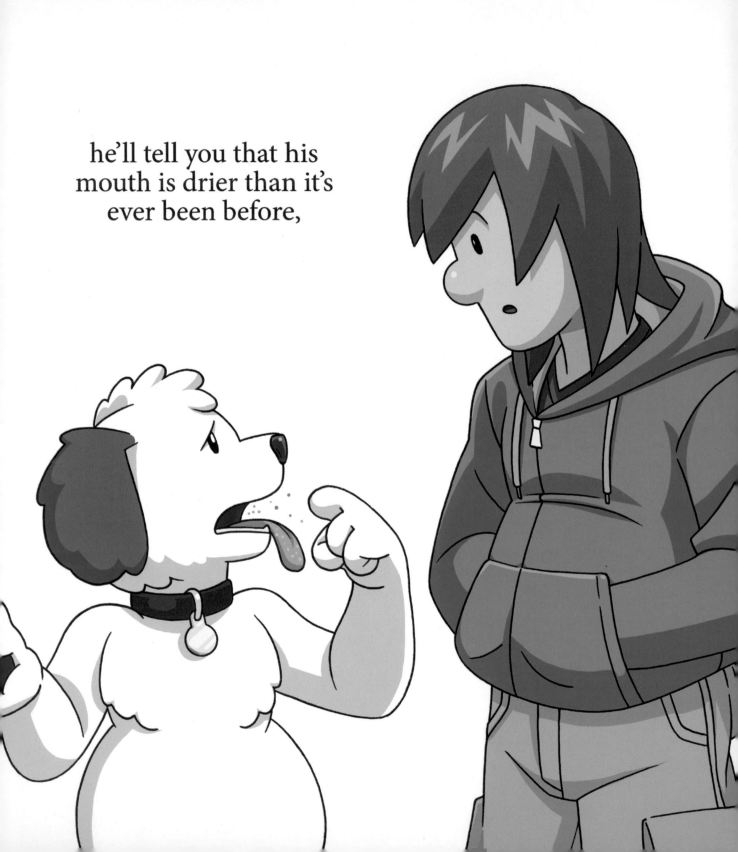

he'll tell you that his mouth is drier than it's ever been before,

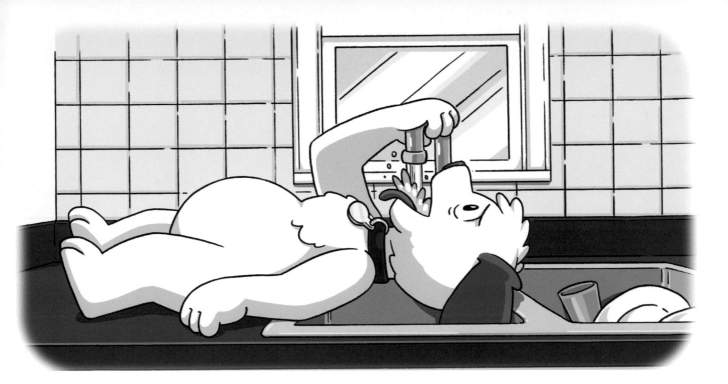

and that he's never been
so thirsty in his life.

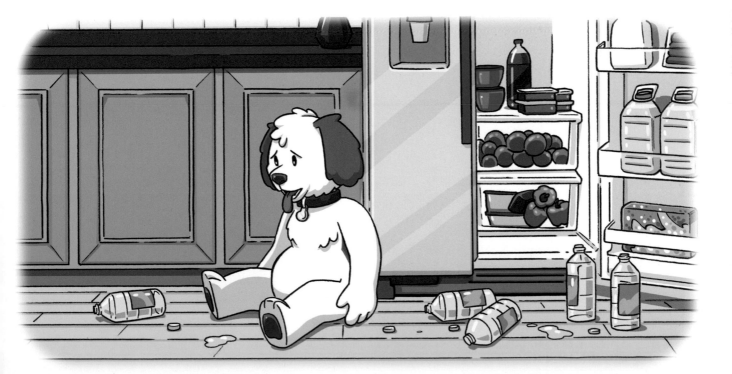

The skull and crossbones
in the fish tank will remind him of
the treats he gets at home.

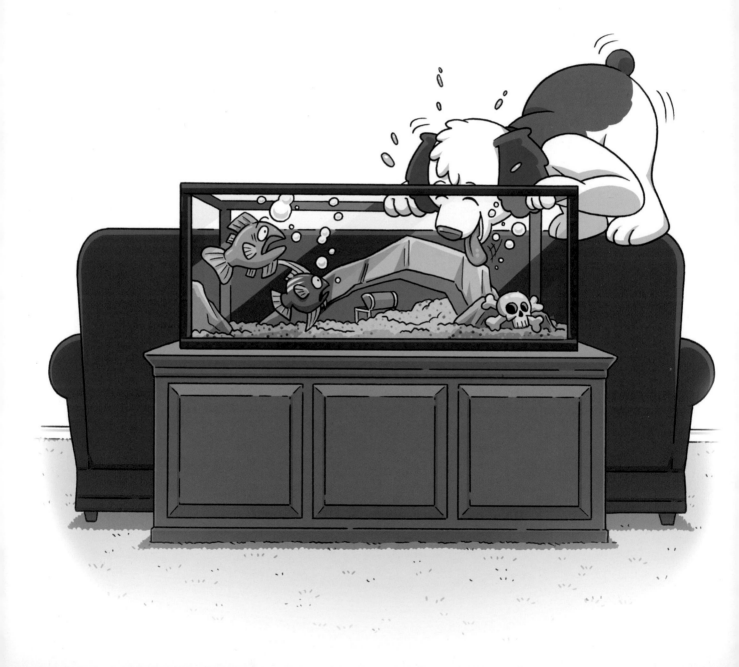

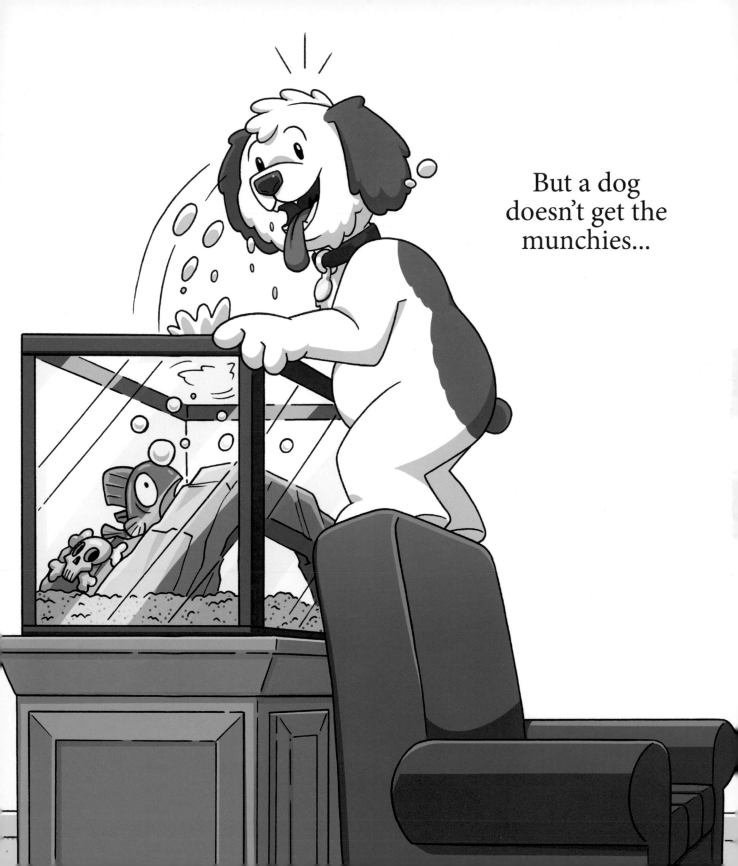

But a dog
doesn't get the
munchies...

He gets the chewies!

He'll be amazed at how much the shoelaces look like ramen noodles, and he'll ask you to take him to the store to buy some.

When he tells you that
flying down the road with
the wind in his face is the
best feeling ever,

you'll tell him the car's
still in the driveway.
YOTA
28IF

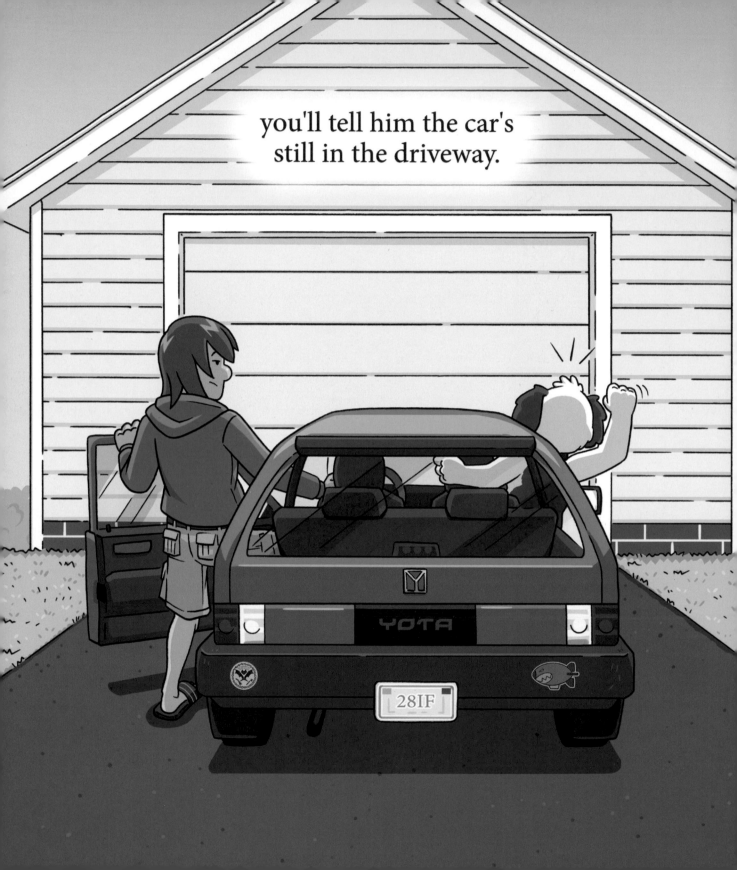

At the store, he'll ask you
to buy him catnip...

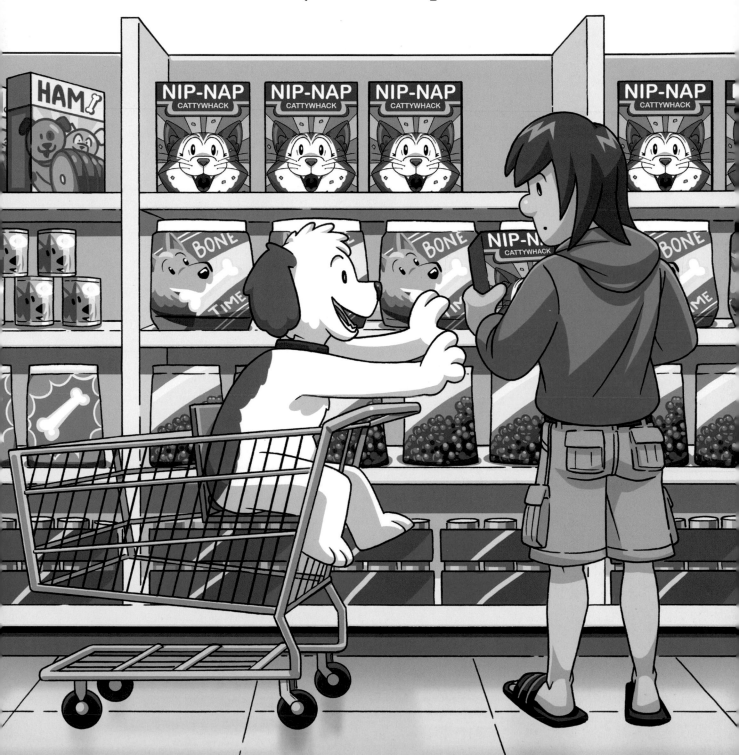

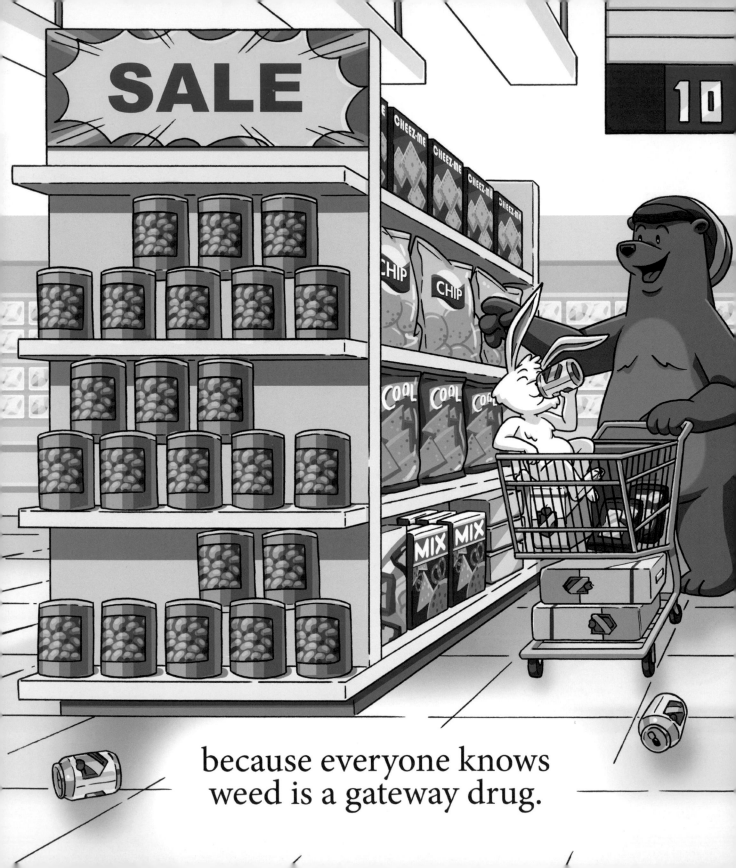

because everyone knows
weed is a gateway drug.

GIFT CARDS
PHARMACY
NIP-NAP
CATTYWHACK

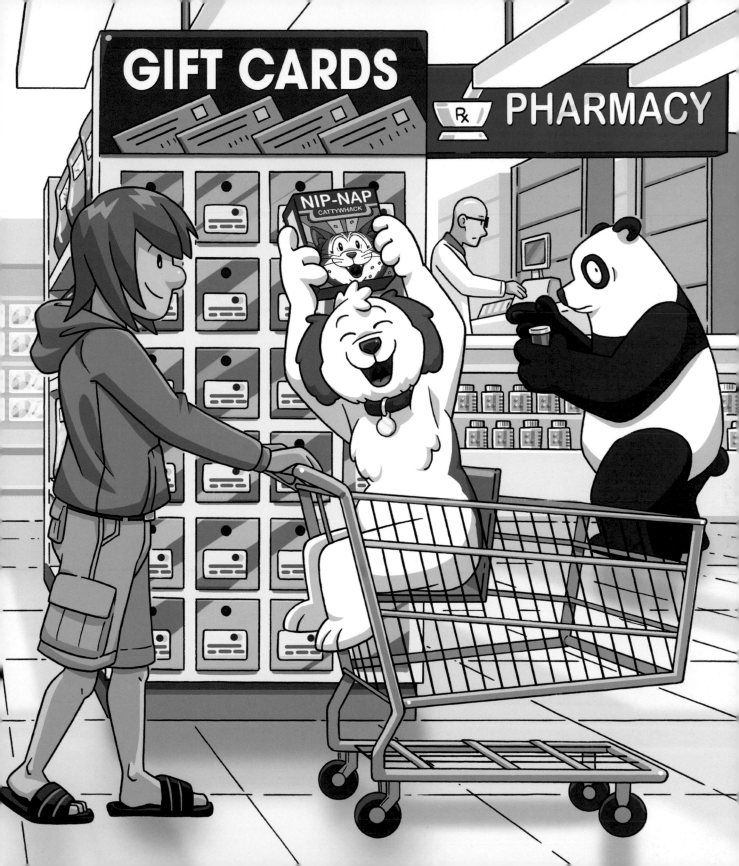

When he asks you
to stop and get tacos
on the way home,

you'll remind him that
you already did.
Talbott's
Tacos

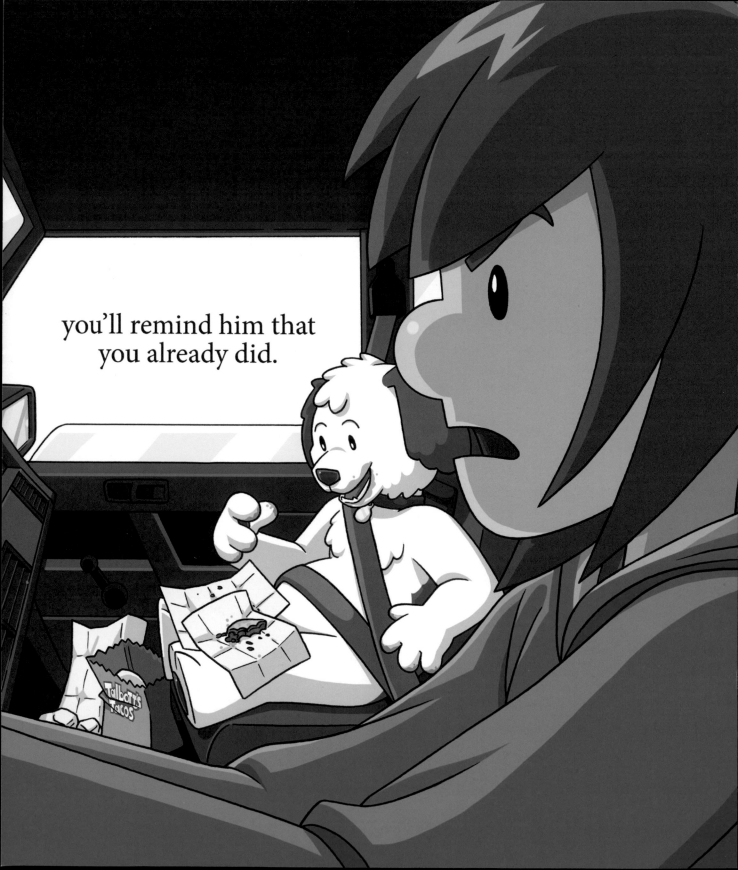

When you get to
a stop sign, he'll tell
you to hold on...

STOP
YOTA
28IF

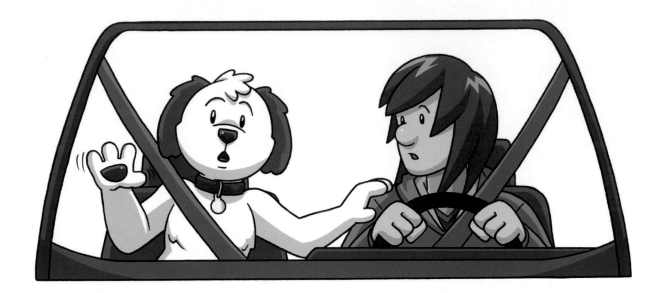

you've got to wait for
it to turn green.

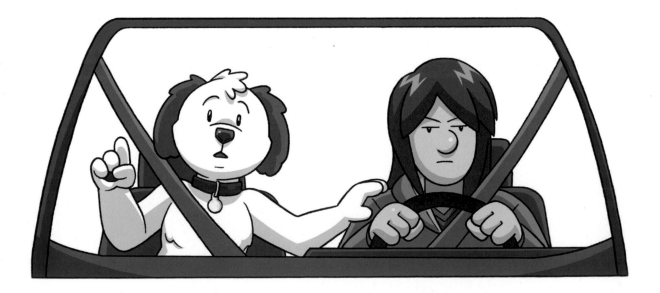

28IF

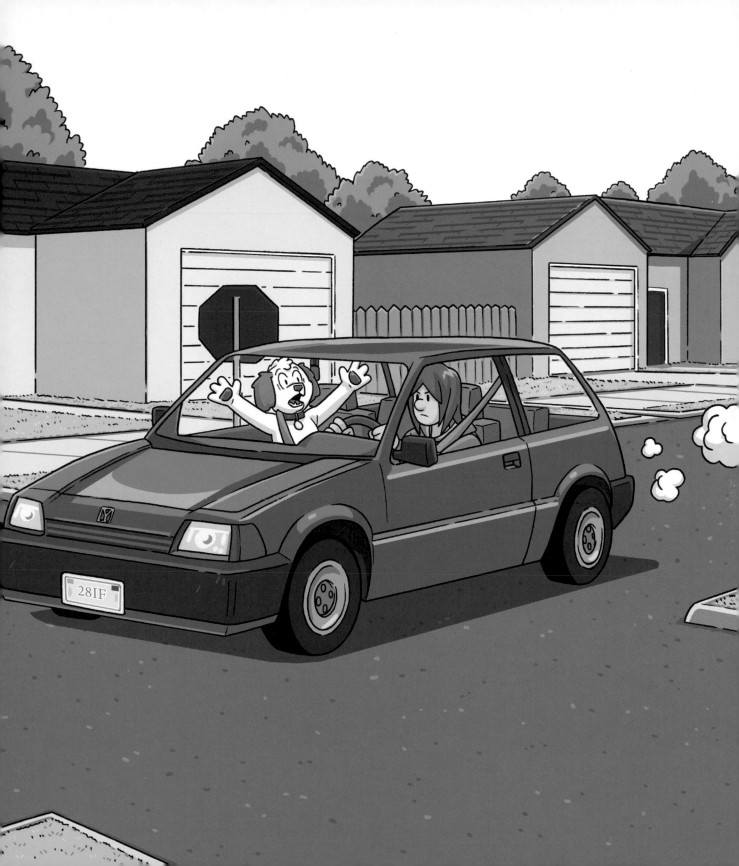

NIP-NAP
CATTYWHACK

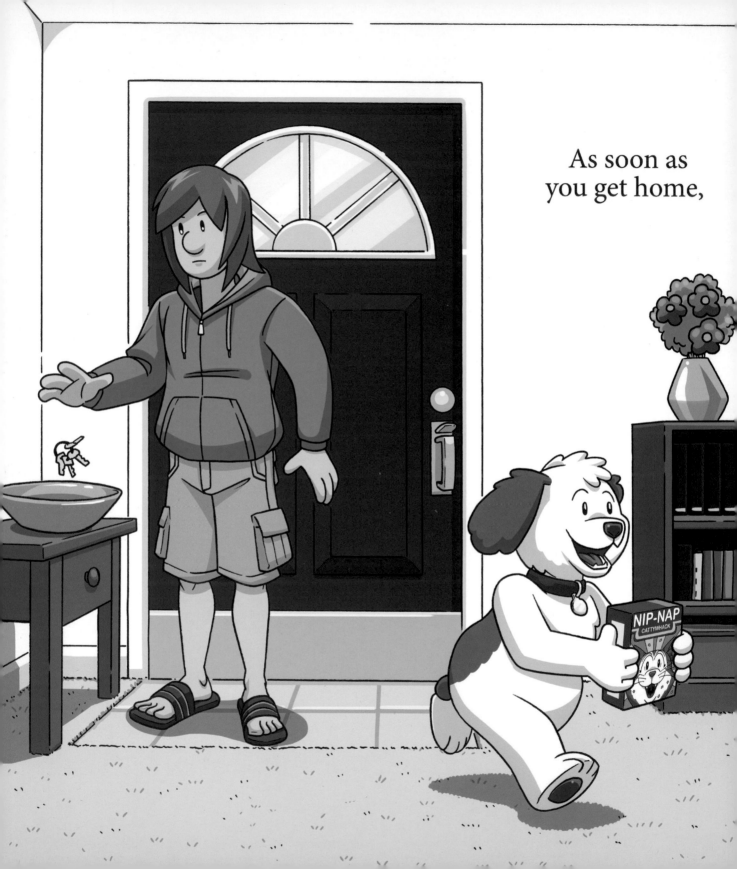

As soon as
you get home,

he'll want to try
the catnip.

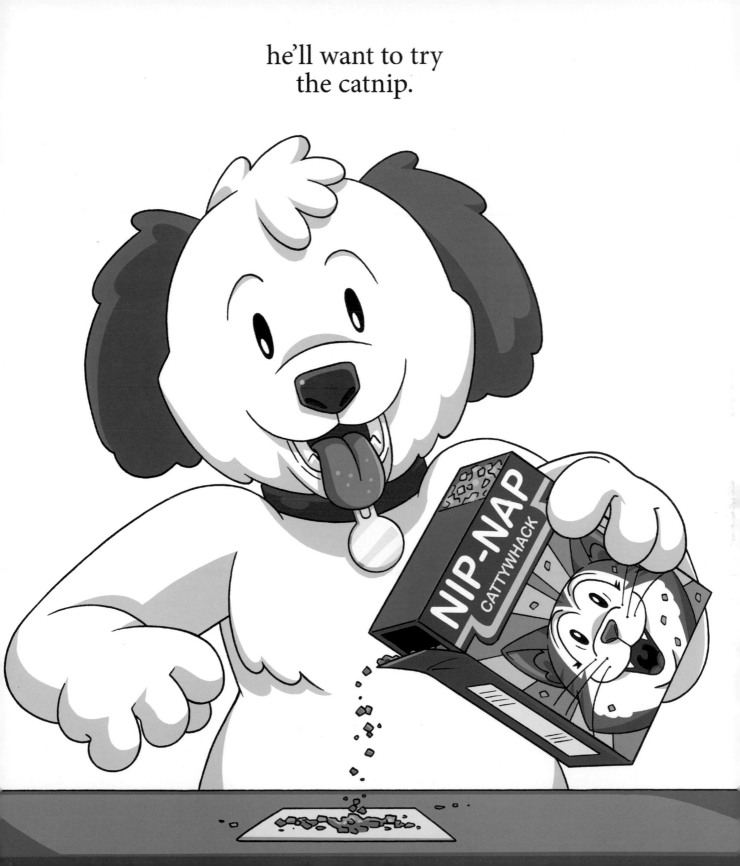

Then he'll play...

And play...

And play...

Until...

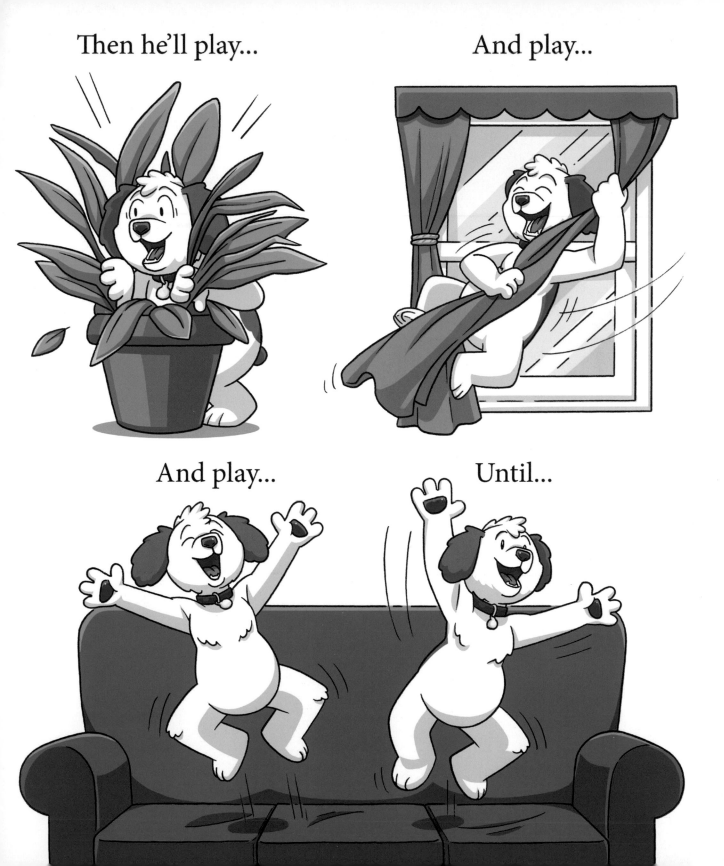

he can't play
anymore.

Z Z Z Z
NIP-NAP

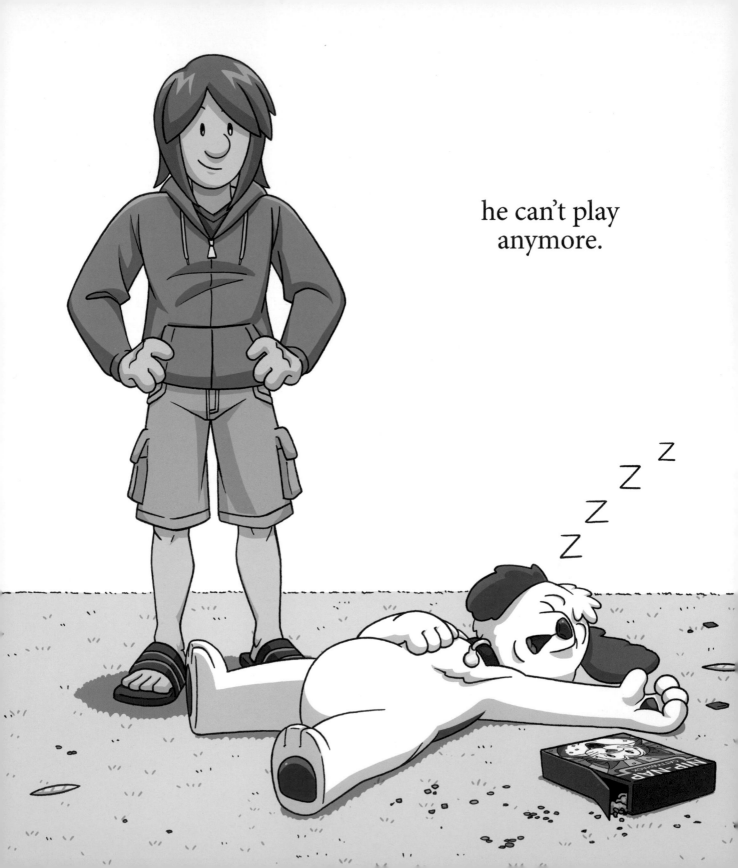

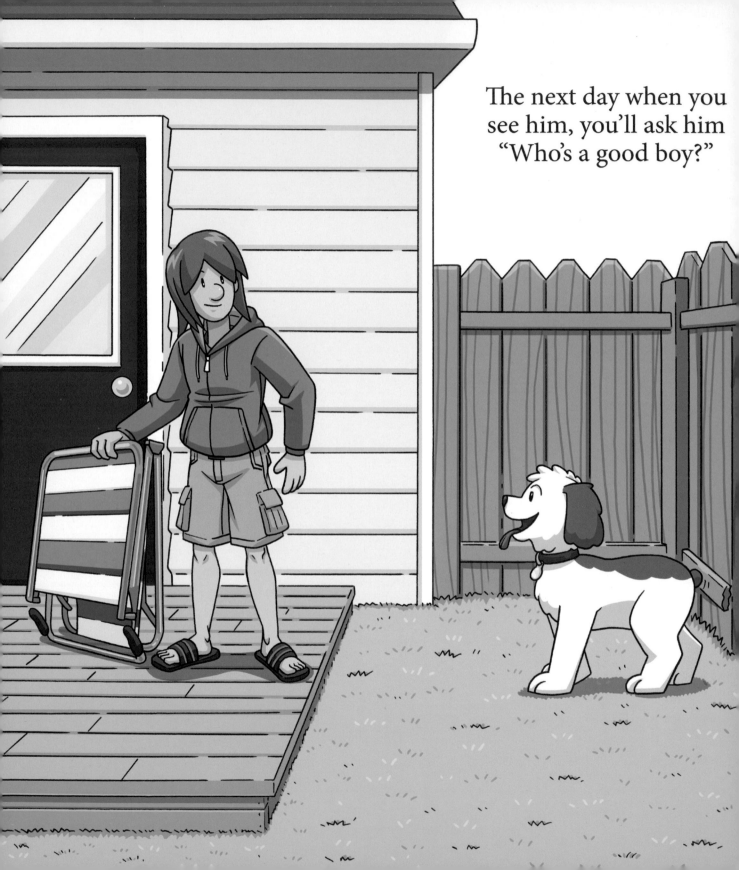

The next day when you see him, you'll ask him "Who's a good boy?"

He'll tell you
he is...

But he's not.

All rights reserved. No part of this book may be reproduced in any manner without the express written consent of the publisher, except in the case of brief excerpts in critical reviews or articles. All inquiries should be addressed to Skyhorse Publishing, 307 West 36th Street, 11th Floor, New York, NY 10018.

Skyhorse Publishing books may be purchased in bulk at special discounts for sales promotion, corporate gifts, fund-raising, or educational purposes. Special editions can also be created to specifications. For details, contact the Special Sales Department, Skyhorse Publishing, 307 West 36th Street, 11th Floor, New York, NY 10018 or info@skyhorsepublishing.com.

Skyhorse® and Skyhorse Publishing® are registered trademarks of Skyhorse Publishing, Inc.®, a Delaware corporation.

Visit our website at www.skyhorsepublishing.com.

10 9 8 7 6 5 4 3 2

Library of Congress Cataloging-in-Publication Data is available on file

Cover and interior artwork by Mike Odum

Print ISBN: 978-1-5107-6101-8

E-book ISBN: 978-1-5107-6595-5

Printed in China

Also Available

A PARODY BOOK
The Addicted Animal Series
If You Give A Bunny A Beer
WRITTEN BY
Sam Miserendino
ILLUSTRATED BY
Mike Odum
(Serif New Red)

A PARODY BOOK
The Addicted Animal Series
If You Give A Bear A Bong
WRITTEN BY
Sam Miserendino
ILLUSTRATED BY
Mike Odum

A PARODY BOOK
The Addicted Animal Series
If You Give A Kitty A Cocktail
WRITTEN BY
Sam Miserendino
ILLUSTRATED BY
Mike Odum

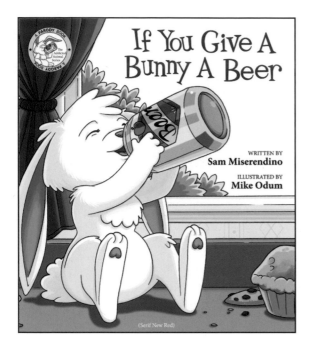

Humor

US $12.99/Can $17

The fourth installment in Sam Miserendino and Mike Odum's Addicted Animal series

Following the success of other adult-themed parodies of children's books, author Sam Miserendino presents a delightful tale that will entertain readers with its charming combination of innocence and lack thereof. A humorous play off of the famous *If You Give a Moose a Muffin*, *If You Give a Dog a Doobie* tells the tale of a pot-loving pooch whose toking neighbor gives him the best treat ever. The book follows the dog as he experiences the highs and lows of being high and reveals whether or not it's possible to teach a stoned dog new tricks … or to even get him to remember old ones!

Featuring hilarious full-color illustrations by Mike Odum, this heartwarming cautionary tale informs readers of the dangers of mixing pot and pups.

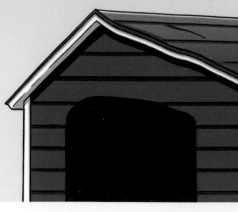

SAM MISERENDINO is an attorney by day, author by night, and father 24/7. It was in this latter role that Sam was inspired to write about cocktail-drinking kitties and bong-smoking bears. After reading books about carb-addicted moose, mice, and pigs to his son and daughter for the millionth time, Sam's thoughts drifted to other animals with other addictions. Sam lives in Buffalo, New York, with his wife, two children, two dogs, and two cats, none of whom, he is happy to report, are addicted to anything more serious than chew toys, catnip, and television.

MIKE ODUM is a former bartender, so he has extensive experience with inebriated mammals. Mike's observation of bar fauna informed his skillful renderings in *If You Give A Bunny a Beer* and *If You Give A Bear A Bong*. When not drawing drunken cats and stoned bears, Mike develops games for ROOT 76——a game company he cofounded. Mike lives in Richmond, Virginia, with his wife and two-year-old daughter, who enjoys sneaking into his studio and adding her own touches to his work.

Also Available

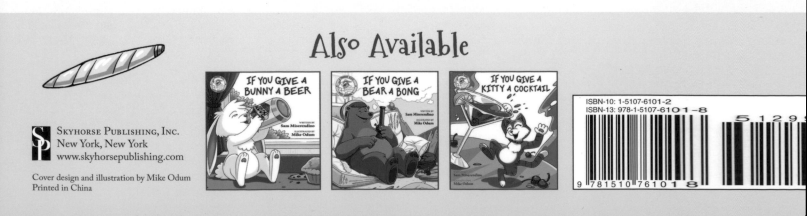

Skyhorse Publishing, Inc.
New York, New York
www.skyhorsepublishing.com

Cover design and illustration by Mike Odum
Printed in China

ISBN-10: 1-5107-6101-2
ISBN-13: 978-1-5107-6101-8

9 781510 761018